PHONICS FOR SPELLING

Children's Reading & Writing Education Books

All Rights reserved. No part of this book may be reproduced or used in any way or form or by any means whether electronic or mechanical, this means that you cannot record or photocopy any material ideas or tips that are provided in this book.

Copyright 2016

PRACTICE SPELLING WITH PHONICS

LEVEL 1

SPELLING NO. 1

Write the missing letters of each word (br, dr, tr).

___own   ___um

SPELLING NO. 2

Write the missing letters of each word (tr, bl, kr).

____ocks   ____ain

SPELLING NO. 3

Write the missing letters of each word (dr, cr, fr).

____ab   ____uits

SPELLING NO. 4

Write the missing letters of each word (cl, bl, fl).

_____oud   _____y

SPELLING NO. 5

Write the missing letters of each word (ch, th, gh).

____ain   swit____

SPELLING NO. 6

Write the missing letters of each word (sh, ch, gh).

___ark   tra___

SPELLING NO. 7

Write the missing letters of each word (th, gh, wh).

____ree   ____eel

SPELLING NO. 8

Write the missing letters of each word (gh, th, ph).

ear____   lau____

SPELLING NO. 9

Write the missing letters of each word (ea, ch, oa).

____eese   b____t

SPELLING NO. 10

Write the missing letters of each word (ea, cl, oe).

____ean   backh____

SPELLING NO. 11

Write the missing letters of each word (sc, oo, gr).

____ass   ____ale

SPELLING NO. 12

Write the missing letters of each word (sk, bl, gl).

____ove   ____ate

SPELLING NO. 13

Write the missing letters of each word (pr, tr, sl).

___etzel   ___ipper

SPELLING NO. 14

Write the missing letters of each word (pl, sm, gl).

___ug   ___ock

SPELLING NO. 15

Write the missing letters of each word (ch, zi, ph).

___oto   wat___

SPELLING NO. 16

Write the missing letters of each word (kn, sm, ng).

____ife   ri____

PRACTICE SPELLING WITH PHONICS

LEVEL 2

SPELLING NO. 1

Write the missing letter of each word (p, e).

1.  __lan__

2.  sh__e__

3.  Zi__p__r

SPELLING NO. 2

Write the missing letter of each word (k, q, i ,).

1.  __uail

2.  k__ng

3.  duc__

SPELLING NO. 3

Write the missing letter of each word (c, d, n ,).

1.    d_lphi__

2.    __an__le

3.    spoo__

SPELLING NO. 4

Write the missing letter of each word (j, b, i ,).

1.  __am

2.  __oat

3.  __gloo

SPELLING NO. 5

Write the missing letter of each word (k, a, t).

1.  h__t

2.  an__

3.  boo__

SPELLING NO. 6

Write the missing letter of each word (f, o, l ,).

1.  U__ __

2.  __r__g

3.  __ea__

SPELLING NO. 7

Write the missing letter of each word (o, t, k,).

1.  s__ c__

2.  g__ a__

3.  j__ __er

SPELLING NO. 8

Write the missing letter of each word (h, o, t,).

1.    t__ma__o

2.    ho__d__g

3.   __ __ use

SPELLING NO. 9

Write the missing letter of each word (r, h, k ,).

1.    __eyboa__d

2.    wo__m

3.    ca__e

SPELLING NO. 10

Write the missing letter of each word (e, l, n ,).

1.    e__epha__t

2.    p__ngui__

3. __mbre__la

SPELLING NO. 11

Write the missing letter of each word (a, r).

1.  c_p

2.  v__ltu__e

3.  k__nga__oo

SPELLING NO. 12

Write the missing letter of each word (e, u, i).

1.  b __ e

2.  m __ shroom

3.  p __ ncil

SPELLING NO. 13

Write the missing letter of each word (I, i).

1.  __ce cream

2.  is__and

3.  g__obe

SPELLING NO. 14

Write the missing letter of each word (r, l, a).

1.    yogu__t

2.    __nima__s

3.    g__andm__

SPELLING NO. 15

Write the missing letter of each word (l, m, e ,).

1.  f__ow__r

2.  __e__on

3.  grap__s

ANSWERS

Level I

SPELLING NO. 1
brown
drum

SPELLING NO. 2
blocks
train

SPELLING NO. 3
crab
fruits

SPELLING NO. 4
cloud
fly

SPELLING NO. 5
chain
switch

SPELLING NO. 6
shark
trash

SPELLING NO. 7
three
wheel

SPELLING NO. 8
earth
laugh

SPELLING NO. 9
cheese
boat

SPELLING NO. 10
clean
backhoe

SPELLING NO. 11
grass
scale

SPELLING NO. 12
glove
skate

SPELLING NO. 13
pretzel
zipper

SPELLING NO. 14
plug
smock

SPELLING NO. 15
photo
wash

SPELLING NO. 16
knife
ring

Level 2

SPELLING NO. 1
1. plane
2. sheep
3. Zipper

SPELLING NO. 2
1. quail
2. king
3. duck

SPELLING NO. 3
1. dolphin
2. candle
3. spoon

SPELLING NO. 4
1. jam
2. goat
3. igloo

SPELLING NO. 5
1. hat
2. ant
3. book

SPELLING NO. 6
1. UFO
2. frog
3. leaf

SPELLING NO. 7
1. sock
2. goat
3. joker

SPELLING NO. 8
1. tomato
2. hotdog
3. house

SPELLING NO. 9
1. keyboard
2. worm
3. cake

SPELLING NO. 10
1. elephant
2. penguin
3. umbrella

SPELLING NO. 11
1. cap
2. vulture
3. kangaeoo

SPELLING NO. 12
1. bee
2. mushroom
3. pencil

SPELLING NO. 13
1. Ice cream
2. island
3. globe

SPELLING NO. 14
1. yogurt
2. animals
3. grandma

SPELLING NO. 15
1. flower
2. lemon
3. grapes

You did great!
With the Exercises!

www.ingramcontent.com/pod-product-compliance
Lightning Source LLC
LaVergne TN
LVHW082254070426
835507LV00037B/2288